SAINT JOHN THE SHORT & THE TREE OF OBEDIENCE

A BOOK ABOUT OBEDIENCE FOR TODDLERS AND YOUNG CHILDREN

BY CREATIVE ORTHODOX

© CREATIVE ORTHODOX, 2024 ALL RIGHTS RESERVED.
ONLY THE COPYRIGHT HOLDER MAY PRODUCE AND SELL PRINTED AND ELECTRONIC VERSIONS OF THIS WORK.

WHO LOVES TO SERVE, LOVES TO PRAY, AND HELPS WHENEVER HE CAN.

"BUT A MONK WHO IS PROUD IS A DANGEROUS ONE, SO I HAVE TO PUT HIM TO THE TEST."

THEY HIKE AND MARCH, AND SHUFFLE AND WALK,
'TIL THE SUN STARTS HURTING THEIR HEADS!

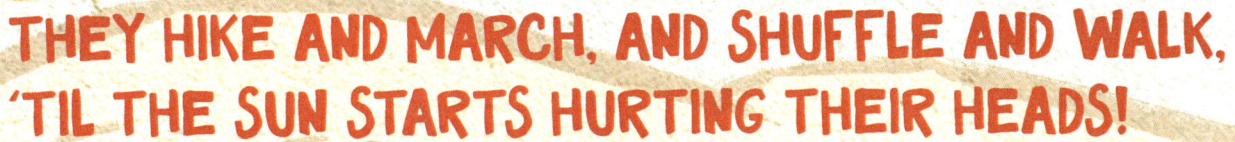

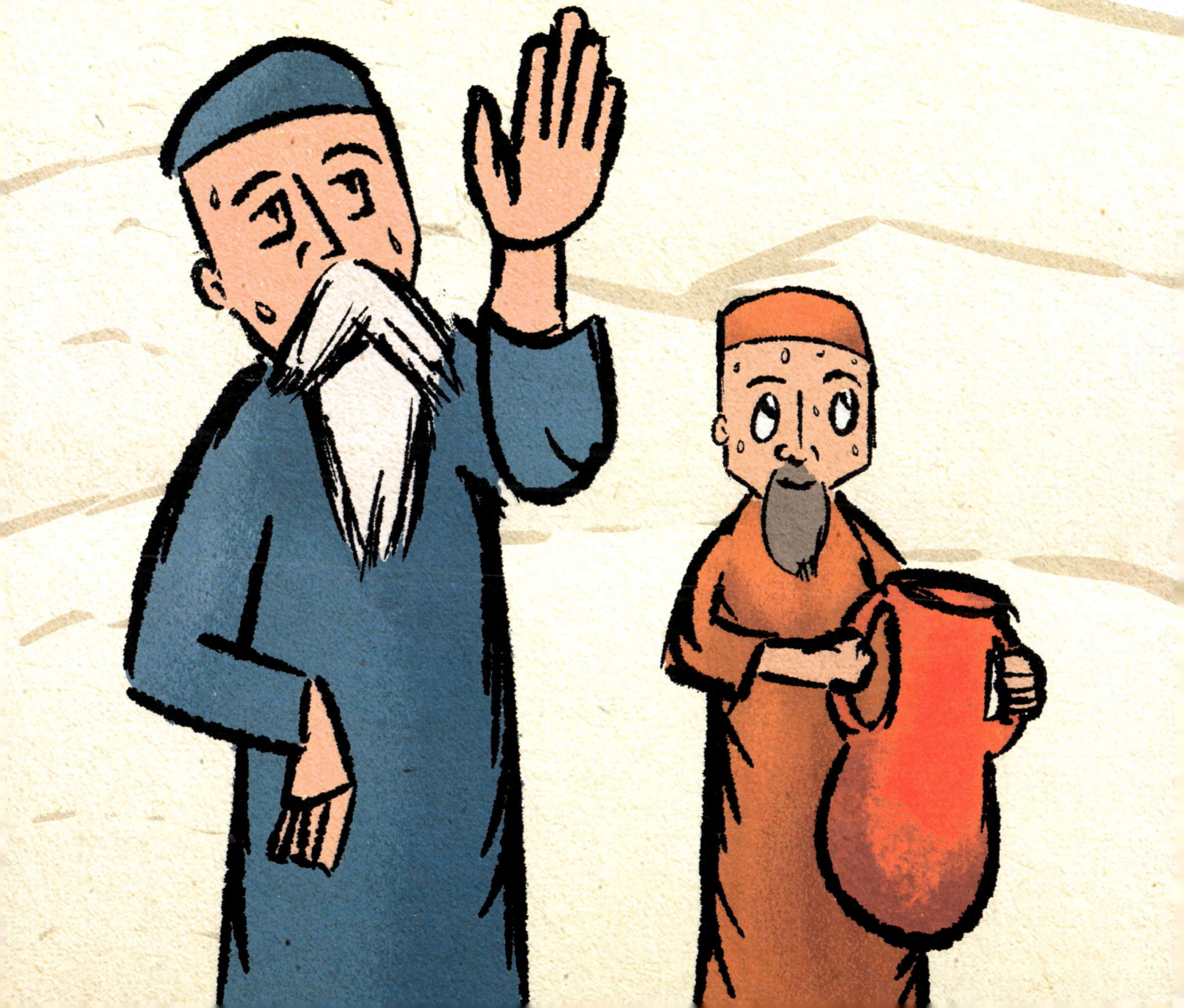

HE GRABS A DEAD STICK,
AND JOHN FOLLOWS QUICK,
WITH A BUCKET OF WATER IN HAND.

JOHN KNOWS THAT ALL TREES,
GROW ONLY FROM SEEDS,
AND A STICK THAT IS DEAD DOESN'T GROW.

BUT CHOOSES TO DO WHAT HIS ABBA HAD ASKED, AS OBEDIENCE IS ALL THAT HE KNOWS.

SO JOHN WAKES UP,
AND WALKS TO THE WELL,
AND FILLS UP HIS JUG BEFORE THE SUNRISE.

HE DOES IT WITH LOVE AND DOES IT WITH CARE,
FOR DAYS AND MONTHS, AND YEARS HE DOES SO.

A PRAYER

DEAR SAINT JOHN THE SHORT,

PRAY FOR US TO BE OBEDIENT LIKE YOU,
TO GOD, OUR PARENTS AND OUR FAMILY TOO.
PRAY THAT WE GROW IN VIRTUE AND GRACE,
LIKE THE DRY STICK AND THE TREE
THAT GREW IN ITS PLACE!

AMEN.

ABOUT SAINT JOHN THE SHORT:

SAINT JOHN THE SHORT LIVED A LONG TIME AGO IN A MONASTERY IN THE EGYPTIAN DESERT. HE WANTED TO BE LIKE THE HOLY MONKS SAINT ANTONY AND SAINT MACARIUS, SO HE BECAME A MONK TOO.

A STRICT TEACHER NAMED AMOI TOOK JOHN AS HIS DISCIPLE. JOHN LEARNED IMPORTANT LESSONS ABOUT HUMILITY, FAITH, AND OBEDIENCE. OVER TIME, HE BECAME A WISE DESERT FATHER AND HELPED MANY OTHER MONKS GROW IN THEIR FAITH.

THANK YOU.

I APPRECIATE YOU BUYING AND READING CREATIVE ORTHODOX BOOKS. I PRAY YOU AND YOUR LITTLE ONES ENJOY THEM AND FIND THEM EDIFYING. PLEASE USE THIS COUPON AT CHECKOUT TO GET 10% OFF YOUR NEXT ORDER: **CREATIVE10**

VISIT **CREATIVEORTHODOX.COM/ACTIVITIES** FOR **FREE** PRINTABLES FOR YOUR LITTLE ONES!

IF YOU'D LIKE TO LEARN MORE ABOUT SAINT JOHN THE SHORT, CHECK OUT MY GRAPHIC NOVEL "A FOREST IN THE DESERT" FOR AGES 10+.

MICHAEL ELGAMAL IS A CANADIAN EGYPTIAN WRITER AND ARTIST. HE STARTED CREATIVE ORTHODOX TO TELL STORIES OF ANCIENT CHRISTIANITY. MICHAEL LIVES IN ONTARIO, CANADA WITH HIS LITTLE FAMILY.

www.ingramcontent.com/pod-product-compliance
Lightning Source LLC
Chambersburg PA
CBRC091724070526
44585CB00008B/164